Why I Left Judaism

Why I Left Judaism
A Candid and Humorous Look

Esther Elisheva Steinberg

The Hermit Kingdom Press
Cheltenham ★ Seoul ★ Bangalore ★ Cebu

WHY I LEFT JUDAISM:
A CANDID AND HUMOROUS LOOK

Copyright © 2004 by Esther Elisheva Steinberg

All rights reserved. No part of this book may be reproduced in any form or by any means, electronic or mechanical, including photocopying, recording, or by any information storage and retrieval system, without permission in writing from the publisher.

ISBN 1-59689-002-9

Write-To Address:

The Hermit Kingdom Press
3741 Walnut Street, Suite 407
Philadelphia, PA 19104
United States of America

Info@TheHermitKingdomPress.com

Hermit Kingdom
12 South Bridge, Suite 370
Edinburgh, EH1 1DD
Scotland

http://www.TheHermitKingdomPress.com

"In reality, the fact of being is what is most private; existence is the sole thing I cannot communicate; I can tell about it, but I cannot share my existence."

Emmanuel Levinas

Contents

Reason One: Jewish Men <9>

Reason Two: The Image <19>

Reason Three: The Religion <27>

Reason Four: The Jewish State <41>

Reason One:

Jewish Men

Call me a silly gal and slap me silly, but for a girl, Jewish or not, men are important. And let's face it – Jewish men are not the sexiest men in the world.

Am I wrong or am I wrong? Jewish men are – how should I put it – mama's boys. Don't get me wrong, it's not an insult on the Jewish mamas. They are the best in the world.

But do Jewish men have to be the way they are? Should we blame the loving Jewish mamas for how they are?

I say, give credit to the Jewish moms. They love their children and pour their energy raising them.

So, who should take responsibility for the way Jewish men are the way they are? The Jewish men, of course.

Now, now, don't go blaming your Yiddish mamas for the way you turned out.

You know what I mean.

All Jewish women know.

You have to take responsibility.

For me, I guess I can crusade to reform the Jewish men. But let me just say that I don't much feel like engaging in that crusade.

It's not my mission. And who can stand the stress? I don't want to hate raising children even before I have ones of my own.

So, what's the solution?

Let the Jewish men be. Let them find their masculinity. Let them figure out what it means to be men. Let them search a way to escape from their mama's boy-ness.

I am just not going to be there to watch it all happen.

Who has the time?

There's shopping to be done, pretty clothes to buy, good movies to see, nice concerts to attend, and enjoy life.

I want to find happiness.

And let's face it. Jewish men are getting in the way.

Every time, Jewish men find out I am Jewish, they go all Yiddish on me. They expect me to live up to the standards they set, based on their mamas.

I can't take it any more.

So, I'm renouncing my Jewishness. I am abandoning Judaism – in all forms.

No Jewish man will be able to say, "You are Jewish!" Ever again!

Yes. I am throwing away my Jewishness.

And Jewish men are to blame – well, at least in part.

I know I will be happier.

I could date men who are like real men. Jewish men just do not fit the bill. Yes, it's just my opinion. But it's like common knowledge in the Jewish girly circles.

Non-Jewish men tend to be more masculine. They even look more masculine. And they act like real men – not like mama's boys.

Abandoning Judaism makes me feel free. I won't have the pressure to marry someone who's Jewish.

I had my portion of Jewish group guilt trip. Not marrying a Jew is like genocide. What Nazis could not accomplish through the death camps,

Jewish girls do it by marrying non-Jews. Blah, blah, blah.

Who needs the guilt trip?

You see. If I am not Jewish, I won't need to feel guilty for liking and even marrying a non-Jewish man.

If Jewish men were more like men, I guess I might have been persuaded to remain Jewish. But they are not – certainly in my eyes.

Abandoning Judaism, I will feel no guilt as I date and find the man (not mama's boy!) of my dreams.

You may think that I have a very Jewish name. Okay. You are right. It can't get more Jewish than that. So, I guess I'll have to change my full name.

One step at a time, now.

It's only recent that I made the decision to leave Judaism.

I am not a Jew!

How liberating it is to say.

I didn't do anything Jewish any way. I am like anybody living here. And I was given my name. It's not like I took the name for myself.

I will give myself a name that will go with my identity.

Why I Left Judaism

Am I rambling? It's just the flood of emotions, you know.

It's excitement, anticipation, and, I guess, fear all rolled up into one, like the cigarettes that some Europeans make on their own with a piece of paper, tobacco, and whatever they want to put in as well – like mint, I guess.

Talking about Europe, look at those European men. They are very masculine. Independent and not attached to their moms through an emotional umbilical cord.

Take Holland for instance.

Those non-Jewish Europeans are very independent. They are almost rude to their women. Okay, they are not rude. They are polite. But they are coldly polite.

15

Perhaps because I am used to the way Jewish men are (and I don't like it!), I am attracted to the cold politeness of non-Jewish Dutch men. But please, please keep me away from all Jewish Dutch men. They are worse than American Jewish men. I am going for purely non-Jewish men, Dutch or otherwise.

And how about those Germans? Okay, okay. It may be anti-Jewish to celebrate German men. But it's not like these German men killed my mother. I don't know any one who was killed by the Nazis, personally. Anyhow, aren't all the Nazis dead?

Let's face it, girls. German men are real men. In fact, their whole Nazi image is quite attractive. Don't get me wrong. I don't like the killing. I don't like all that Aryan stuff.

But the bad boy factor is a turn-on. You know what I mean? And whenever those Nazi documentaries come on, the Nazi soldiers are so manly that a Jewish girl cannot but be tickled pink. It comes with being surrounded by mama's boys one's whole life.

German men are like a breath of fresh air.

And the best thing about it is that German men are still manly, manly, but without all the Nazi distractions.

You know, they still have that bad boy element in them. You know what I mean?

Maybe, to celebrate my new identity, I'll take a trip to Germany. Bavaria, preferably. German men are very masculine, but Bavarians, particularly.

October Fest, here I come!

Reason Two:

The Image

Call me shallow, but image is important to me. As the saying goes, "Image is everything."

And let's face it. Being Jewish isn't the coolest thing in the world.

I know, I may be offending the woman who gave birth to me and the father who labored to keep me sound, healthy, and with many pairs of shoes.

But the word, "Jew," does not inspire warm, fuzzy feelings. Even Jews don't find fellow Jews warm and fuzzy.

Jewish sense of humor is cutting each other down. Compare that with the nice Ned Flanders-like neighbors down the street. They are always so positive. They are so warm. So fuzzy.

Being Jewish is associated with being cheap. Okay, we share that image with the Dutch. But certainly, we have a big claim on the stereotype.

Okay. Maybe there's some truth to it. After all, stereotypes have to come from somewhere. And there is something generally true in them to make the stereotypes (both positive and negative) stick.

The problem is if you are the exception to the rule. You still get dragged down by the stereotype.

One good thing about being Jewish is that it's not like being Dutch. You cannot refuse to be Dutch.

But you can refuse to be Jewish.

What's being a Jew after all? It may be a combination of factors, but it's something that you can easily abandon.

Don't go to synagogue. Don't do anything Jewish. Don't call yourself Jewish. Maybe convert to another religion. And voila! You are not Jewish anymore.

What can be simpler?

It's a benefit for Jews that many others don't have the luxury of having. And I am thankful for that.

And I choose to practice my privilege. Heck, I may even convert to Christianity.

What's so bad about Christianity? Some Jews think it's the Black Plague or something.

A religion that preaches loving neighbors and doing good things doesn't seem like such an evil religion to me.

And in the good o' US of A, being a Christian has so many benefits.

It certainly ups your image. Maybe the fact that most of the people in America are Christians has something to do with it.

Definitely, being a Christian is better for one's image than being a Jew.

Why should I not give Christianity a chance? It's not like I believe in Judaism.

What am I saying? I have left Judaism, so I can explore whatever I want.

I can engage in proper image creation for myself. It'll be doing a lot of good for me.

And it's time to think about me, myself, and I. If I can create a good image for myself, I can do a lot of good things for others.

If I have a bad image, I won't get anywhere.

Leaving Judaism gives me the opportunity to find the right image for myself. I can do a lot of good for myself and others.

I've only begun, baby!

My future is there to be drawn on.

Reason Three:

The Religion

Why I Left Judaism

It's not like I'm trying to offend other Jews. But let's face it, Judaism is not the nicest religion in the world.

Certainly, the intolerance that I see in the Jewish religion fuelled the speed with which I renounced my Jewishness.

Where do I start?

Okay. Let's start here. For a religion that seems to condemn the Nazis, Judaism celebrates genocidal wars.

In the Book of Exodus, Egypt's first-born were killed.

Joshua waged genocidal war against the Canaanites.

Doesn't it seem a bit hypocritical?

I feel like, as long as I remain a Jew, I can't really condemn the Nazis. What's the difference between the Nazis annihilating Jews and the Jews annihilating Canaanites?

I just got attacked by the truth serum. Don't know who put it there. But I have partaken of the fruit of the knowledge of good and evil.

Now, I know. And I can't change that. If I abandon Judaism, I can condemn genocides with a clear conscience.

And I do detest genocides. It's messy and it's very sad.

And how about this idea about the chosen race? It's like the Jewish version of Aryanism.

Jews are a special people because we are chosen. We are somehow more special than everyone else in the world.

We are superior.

I just don't like this kind of talk. It creates unnecessary division between peoples.

And I always hated that girl in elementary school who went around bragging how special she is.

We Jews are doing the same thing by saying that we are special – a chosen race.

I just don't like this superiority talk. I could almost see why people hate us.

All human beings are equal.

I don't like Judaism trying to debunk this important philosophy for the present age.

Thirdly, the tree of the knowledge of good and evil has made me realize fully how anti-women Judaism.

Yes, I have read books written by Jewish women attacking Judaism in this regard. But in the past, I felt a bit offended.

I felt like their criticism of Judaism was a criticism of me. After all, I am Jewish.

Even though I did not believe in the Jewish religion, I felt like I needed to defend Judaism. Somehow, I had been brainwashed into thinking that an attack on Judaism was an attack on me.

Even if it were Jews doing the attacking, I was made to believe that they are self-hating Jews.

Now, I know that I was in a psychological prison.

I am liberating myself from the shackles that bind me.

I am beginning to see that that what the feminists said was true. Judaism is really anti-women.

Take, for instance, the idea that women are impure after menstruation.

Oh, come on! Every woman has menstruation. It's a natural process. It's like this idea created by men to keep women down.

It would have been acceptable thousands of years ago when every other culture was anti-women, but not now.

The disturbing thing is that modern Judaism that observes Jewish law actually upholds this principle. In modern day America, for God's sake!

I am glad that I abandoned Judaism and all the anti-women principles that are so much a part of it.

I choose to leave Judaism and embrace the solidarity of women. Women from all over the world unite!

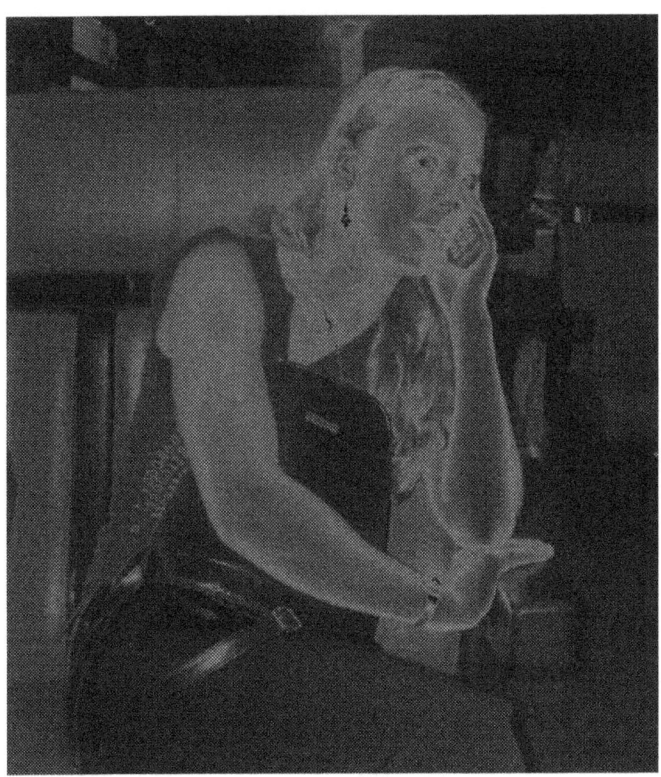

We women can do a lot of good. We are worth so much more than Judaism gives us credit for.

So, I choose to abadon Judaism and embrace a positive future for women, everywhere.

Here's a poem I wrote celebrating women:

"Woman"

I am a woman,
Fragile I may appear,
Helpless you may think,
With no recourse to power.

But you are wrong, you see;
For, I am a woman,
A part of the collective
Woman.

We are all as one,
Sharing destiny
To be one
For the good of all of us.

No anti-woman religion,
Whether it be Judaism
Or Schmudaisim,
Can keep me down.

I am woman,
A part of the collective
Woman,
And hear us roar!

Fourthly, I don't like Judaism because it is always trying to kill people through gratuitous death penalty.

Some of the reasons why people are put to death seem simply ridiculous!

Breaking the Sabbath Day requires the punishment of death penalty?

Come on! You can't be serious!

So, if I drive on Saturday, I should be put to death, if Judaism were faithful to its roots.

It's there clearly in the Hebrew Bible for all to see.

Yes, I can understand (and even support) giving death penalty to someone who brutally raped women against their stated will. Murders who kill a whole family in order to rob them of their wealth should be put to death.

But breaking the Sabbath Day?

It seems like Judaism is really ridiculous.

And its not only the breaking of the Sabbath Day.

The Hebrew Bible seems to be trigger happy in slapping death penalty on people.

Everyone who had premarital sex will have to be put to death, for instance.

Christianity seems much more tolerant. Jesus prevented people from killing a woman caught in adultery by saying that those without sin should throw the first stone.

It seems so much more merciful and loving.

How would you like it if you get caught in a mistake and you will be dealt the full brunt of the death penalty as in the Hebrew Bible?

I rather change my religion. And that's why I'm throwing away the bottle called Judaism and am looking for a replacement.

My fifth reason is kind of related to my fourth reason. I guess it's related in that it highlights the hypocrisy of the fourth reason.

For a religion that seems to dispense the death penalty liberally, it seems to celebrate immorality.

Yes, the adulterous woman should be stoned to death, but, no, Abraham should not be?

Just read through the life of the Patriarchs. Jewish Patriarchs.

Abraham was an immoral guy. He had sex with his wife Sarah's servant.

How would you like it if you hire a nanny for your children and your husband has sex with her?

And Abraham is not alone in the immoral practice.

How about Lot, Abraham's nephew. Lot has sex with his two daughters.

That is just simply sick. And the Hebrew Bible seems to celebrate this incest. Judaism does not seem to condemn such a practice. I don't see the condemnation in there.

And how about King David, the celebrated hero of Judaism. He had sex with a married woman after watching her bathe. She becomes pregnant. King David calls his general, her husband, from battle, to cover up his wrong. When he refuses to have sex with his wife because he said his men are at war, King David sends him out to die, giving specific orders to ensure his death.

And this King David is the hero of Judaism.

I just don't want any part of this kind of a religion. I may be without religion after abandoning Judaism. But I feel being without religion is so much better than having that kind of a religion.

At least I know what morality is.

Reason Four:

The Jewish State

Let me get this right. There are people still going around saying, "The Christian State." No, I didn't think so. It just sounds ridiculous.

So, why isn't it ridiculous to go around saying, "The Jewish State"?

It's such an outdated way to talk.

It's like using black-and-white TV in today's culture of digital color TVs.

It is simply ridiculous.

Why are people holding onto an ideology that was created in the same caldron with Nazism?

A state that must be only for Jews is so not twenty-first century. It's a period where people celebrate differences within a single country.

But no, we Jews have to go around emphasizing a separate state only for Jews.

It just does not feel right.

Why can't non-Jews live in the State of Israel? Isn't it about time that The Law of Return is changed? The law that states that only Jews are allowed to immigrate to Israel seems to be so anti-human rights.

Shouldn't all human beings be treated as equal?

I thought equality was a value to strive for.

Shouldn't non-Jews be allowed to live happily in Israel?

Should not Israel celebrate differences and promote it?

What is all this anti-Arab propaganda coming out of Israel? It's like Israelis think that Arabs are genetically programmed to be terrorists.

It's just disgusting!

Israel should enter the twentieth-first century. And that goes for all Zionists.

And what else do I not like about the idea of a Jewish state?

Let me put it this way: What is there to like?

I am living in the good o' US of A, where everyone is equal under the law. I do not feel any need for a Jewish state.

In vacation time, I rather go to Hawaii than to the unstable land of Israel.

America is a comfortable place to live whereas McDonalds only entered Israel in the 1990s. That qualifies Israel as a Third World in my opinion.

But if I have to pinpoint what annoys me the most about Israel, it will have to be the way that the State of Israel treats Palestinians.

I just feel like saying to the Israelis, "Make love and not war!"

Sending out advanced military helicopters to bomb civilian areas in the Occupied Territories is not my idea of an act of good will.

What are the Israelis going to do – have a perpetual war with the Palestinians, from generation to generation?

Don't the Israelis know that peace is the way?

I guess that's why I like the good o' Itzak. And by Itzak, I mean Prime Minister Itzak Rabin.

Had Itzak not been clipped by an orthodox Jewish law student from Bar Ilan University in Tel Aviv, Israel might have achieved comprehensive peace.

Jews and Arabs could have lived in peace, from generation to generation.

I have to say that the fact that many Jewish rabbis approved such a murder to preserve "the land promised to Abraham" was certainly a factor to doubt the legitimacy of Judaism as a good religion.

Make love, not war.

As much as I condemn what Israel is doing to Palestinians, I condemn with greater ferocity what it is doing to Jews in America.

My gosh! Jewish identity has become tied to the State of Israel. So, every bad thing that Israel does makes American Jews look bad.

Okay, it's unfair to blame only Israel. After all, American Jews have not downplayed the connection.

In fact, some may say that it was the American Jews who worked to forge the strong bond.

We created many multi-million-dollar lobby groups to help Israel.

I guess, I don't object to helping Israel. What I do object to is helping Israel to maintain the oppressive program.

It's like maintaining a fundamentalist regime.

If Israel were more open to peace, it would make American Jews look better.

All that money and energy poured into Israel's interest and what do American Jews get in return?

Most Americans who have a negative perception of Israel translate that sentiment toward Jews.

Negative press is something that I just don't need – especially when I object to human rights abuses by the State of Israel. Why should I suffer for Israel's sins?

So, definitely, what Israel is doing is certainly an important part of the reason why I decided to abandon Judaism.

If Israel were "a light unto the nations," maybe I would not have abandoned Judaism so quickly. But as it stands, Israel is anything but a beacon of light.

Israel does not symbolize peace.

And sentiment is growing in America that seems to be going in the direction of anti-Israel.

Let's face it. The whole world is basically anti-Israel now. They have been for a while.

The United Nations constantly vote against Israel, for God's sake!

Israel should wake up and smell the coffee. The current position is a train track to nowhere.

Israel (and Zionists!) have to realize that in the age of globalization, the concept of the Jewish state is not viable.

Why I Left Judaism

The Jewish state can only do disservice to Jews all over the world by its effort to maintain the purity of Jewishness on a state level.

They say about 50 per cent of Jews in America marry non-Jews.

This alone should be a good indicator of the need to change course.

And I am not alone in abandoning Judaism.

I am not the only one who has turned her back on Jewishness.

I am not unique in desiring not to be identified as a Jew.

More an more young people are thinking like me.

And they share my reasons.

About the Author

Esther Elisheva Steinberg grew up in the East Coast and received an Ivy League education, where she discovered herself. Steinberg continues to be very active on issues affecting Jews.

www.ingramcontent.com/pod-product-compliance
Lightning Source LLC
Chambersburg PA
CBHW032136090426
42743CB00007B/617